# Doubra Fufeyin

## FRIENDSHIP IS LOVE

# Dedication

This book is dedicated to my best friend Omoesiri Lena Pcmu-Omokhaye.
For making me experience the joys of friendship in a deep and overwhelming way. For holding my hand every step of the way, through my experiences good and bad. A symbol of loyalty and sisterhood spanning decades and promising to last forever.

Doubra Fufeyin: Friendship is Love

# THOUGHTS

The journey through life is never complete, especially when you stand alone. There is strength in unity, in sharing your experience with others. There is fulfilment when the love you give is reciprocated. You are more blessed when the love you give is not deserved. The joy is even greater when you are loved for being you and nothing more. A much greater love exists in Christ Jesus who gave up his life and encourages us to do the same.

Doubra Fufeyin.

Doubra Fufeyin: Friendship is Love

## PREFACE

If there is one thing in life which makes everything easier, to me, it is love. It is one thing to find love and another thing altogether to keep it. I have always wondered and pondered on the word love and my answers have never been hard to find.

The saying that charity begins at home comes to mind. As a child, I found it in my immediate surroundings. It was in the countless hugs and kisses and even in the stern warnings of caution as I ran amok in a world where only the simplest things mattered. Like climbing a tree, playing tirelessly in the sand and the streets nearby with other children in the neighbourhood, where every house was a home and every adult was just like mum and dad. It is not the case today and sadly so. There is a look of panic when your eye cannot see your child as he or she plays about in the garden or crosses the street to the ice cream van. The News is a different thing altogether. The fear of what horrors it might bring as the world gets darker, the huge divide between the rich and the poor, the rumours of war and the actual-wars. The declining state of the economy and the (Covid-19) pandemic that is our current plight. The constant killings and issue of lives that matter or do not matter. To me the answer is, still love. Love simply makes the world go round.

Doubra Fufeyin
8 July 2020

Doubra Fufeyin: Friendship is Love

# CONTENTS

Doubra Fufeyin: Friendship is Love

Doubra Fufeyin: Friendship is Love

## TRIBUTE TO SIRI

Over two decades of sisterhood and friendship
that never runs over.
Fine like wine just like honey
better than money.
Ageless, timeless, and priceless.
Mere words cannot quantify or qualify a love
so real and surreal.

I am thankful, I am grateful.
For this gift of inestimable value,
Yes! Like glue we will stick together,
Till our last breath.
No wreaths will justify the beauty of our
journey. I will be there to say this at the very
end as I know you will if the reverse is the case.

That in his life I met someone that I loved.
She was beautiful on the inside
and on the outside.
My Siri, my sister from another mister.
My friend, my pillar, my confidante,
and my greatest advocate.

We have cried, we have laughed,
We have made mistakes from which we learnt.
We became wiser and stronger.

So, after all is said and done.
We came, we bonded, and most
importantly, we loved.

KILBURN STORY

One beautiful day, On my way to Kilburn.
I sat next to this beautiful lady.
A glow on her face with a smile on her lips. She
couldn't hide her joy even if she tried.
I was curious to know and was compelled to
speak.

Since she was in such a good mood, I hoped
that I may be lucky, that she would share.
Penny for your thoughts I said, and this was her
story....
"I am happy." Because the last time I made
this trip, It was blissful. And this is how the story
goes.

"As I made my way on the train and on the
tube to Kilburn, I had a myriad of emotions in
my head. I did not care that I had questions
unanswered. I just was eager to be in a safe
place.
His words were so kind and his touch so warm
and liberating, I didn't know why he wanted
me in his space, but I found myself needing to

be in his space, oblivious to the world and freeing myself to comfort and friendship.

A part of me knew that this time, it would be different. That in Kilburn; I was going to kill and burn my past because the writing was on the wall.

You can lie to everyone but not to yourself. So, I sought solace as he held me, stroked me, and stopped my heart from bleeding that night.

Emotions surged as he told me to keep smiling because my smile was beautiful, that I was beautiful.

I must have talked too much, danced too much and drank too much but it was ok to let loose for the night, because, on this night, I felt strong, I felt like a woman and that was one journey taken that was definitely worth my while".

That is why I am happy" she said, "I am hoping to relieve the magic". "Lucky you" I said, "Maybe I too can find the magic of friendship. Friendship "Makes the world go round"

## I WANT TO SEE

I can't explain but it's plain to see
that, even as the tide, from the sea,
brings messages to the shore,
I am sure there is a reason.

Every season brings a different feeling.
Just as the world goes round.
I go around trying to understand the meaning
of friendship.

I set sail on a ship, bracing myself against the
stormy waters, my heart set on a journey of
discovery.

## FROZEN

There is a stand I have taken, a decision I
am making; to be true to myself or remain
blue. Frozen, but brazen, I challenge myself.
Passions lost they were too fast to leave a
pleasurable mark.

They taunt you with regrets and haunt you like
ghosts from the past. Only the flesh made that
decision. But alas! I found the solution, to

freeze in my stride, only to melt at the touch of Cupid.

THE VOWS

Today, I marry the one I love, the one whose children I will bear. I fear not for I know you will always be near. Now and forever our paths shall never bend. With God it shall never end. With the seal of a kiss, we shall find everlasting bliss.

ALONE IN MY ROOM

Alone in my room, there is a certain gloom.
It evokes emptiness, more like loneliness that
can only be filled with your presence.
If I feel the need to connect with you,
day dreams are my only option.

This is the caption of my exact emotion.
To wish I were in your arms, to wish you were
here to stay.

Most of all, that these

feelings do not fade away with the passage of time. It is a clear message with no ambiguity. Hopefully, it will not be lost in
translation.

## SMOOTH TALKER

The way you talk is like music to my ears. Words that can make any woman melt. Whether you mean is a different thing altogether. If you are a smooth talker, time will tell. You, certainly know how to make a woman feel much more than a woman. A woman and a half. A goddess.

## THIS NEW DAY

This new day gives me the pleasure of realization. Not only have I been disillusioned. I have over the years, built fantasies which like sandcastles are easily eroded.

This new day poses questions. What have I had? Is it what I have always dreamt of? Am I settling for less?
The answer always is that it could be much better.

This new day I shall take a new turn. I wonder why I made so hastily, decisions which later, became omissions.

Now, my mission is to be happier.
I see clearer what I need, what I can achieve and what I will possess.
Better still, it is not so far away.


FRIENDSHIP

It is what brings people together.
It is what makes them happy with each other.
It is what makes them share because they care. They pry, then cry and try to support each other. It is never a bother with each other.

Without friendship imagine how bleak and weak the world would be. Just another blank and empty space. And so, with all the others, let us all stand at peace with each other.

MON AMI

Just because being with you seems natural, just because you see me the way I am and

love me all the same. This is the only reason I
chose to take this path.

I do not know how long it will last but I know
that my shoulder will carry those burdens with
you when night comes. This is the only reason; I
choose to take this path.


HOLIDAY

Sometimes life is like a holiday.
Other times like a hurricane.
Either way, we always wish for a better day.


OH, LITTLE ME OF LITTLE FAITH

In your bosom Oh Lord I seek refuge from the
turbulence around me.
My creator, my friend, the author, and finisher
of my faith.
In my hopelessness and helplessness, you have
shone your light. In my plight, I can see that my
choice is best as I find rest.
Oh, little me of little faith.

In my state of self-pity, I am not empty.
With your blessed assurance I have hope.
In your strength, I have my strength.
In your presence my tent is pitched.
Oh, little me of little faith.

## BY HIS GRACE

By his grace not by my might.
I am what I am. What I profess,
I shall possess through him that strengthens me.

By his grace I shall not fear nor lack; for deep
down in my heart lies the beauty and
greatness of him that strengthens me.

## JUST LIKE FLOWERS

As flowers blossom in spring.
As the crow marks a new day.
As bees make honey.
I have come to realize.
That having you is enough reason to live.

SENSE AND SENSIBILITY

I used to think that I had built a wall where no one could climb or break. I used to think that my heart was immune from pain and hurt. You broke my defenses. Offences, too numerous to mention.

I used your inaction to define your lack of emotion; my inhibitions took over. I dropped my guard and just then you decided to leave, making me question feelings, too numerous to mention.

I used all my power of imagination to lift my heart right back into the equation yet, got no ovation.  All that now seems to be wasted affection, set in the wrong direction, that became a series of afflictions, too numerous to mention.

I used all that was left of my good intention to create a solace from the corruption that spread across my heart, across my body, and across my soul.
Yes, it remains too numerous to mention.

## WORRY NOT

My dear friend.
Let not your face be ruined by worries that
abound. Be gladdened that every step is a
pivot for elevation. The echo of those gone
past is a reminder of what is yet to come.

## BEAUTIFUL TOUCH

The power of touch is a gift. The ability to
create pleasure is a greater gift. But the
greatest is the gift of enjoying pleasure.

## FREEDOM

I long to be free again
Free to live like a child.
Aware of my existence.
Blind to the madness around me.
Be the hunter not the hunted.

I pray not to be a prey of the scavengers.
Who devour at night till there are just bones in
sight. Fly like a bird above the shackles of
human inadequacies, human idiosyncrasies.

Shadowed by the weight of conformity.
Breaking free from it all, to gain the essence of

inner peace. To sweet freedom that is just within sight.

## YOU ARE EVERYWHERE

During the day you are in my thoughts.
During the night you are in my dreams.
My heart needs you to stop bleeding.
I am with you in spirit and it is such a beautiful feeling.

## HEART STRINGS

If there is a way to your heart,
I am on the way to it.
If there is a hole, I will fix it.
If your heart is broken, I will mend it.
If you share this heart with another, you will have my heart to mend.

## THE PROFESSORS AND I

Words are my passion, and this is what I profess. Words are the vessel through which my thoughts come alive. They are
my channel to connect and to be heard.

Words are my voice by choice, my vice, my device, and the price I pay for my pregnant

12

mind. This is my channel to connect and to be heard.

Words are the reason my path has led me to these great ones. Leading me to the ambience of a protégé's garden. This is my channel to connect and to be heard.

Words are your strength they said; you must nurture to mature, if you are to succeed in this world. They emphasized, so I strategized. This is my channel to connect and to be heard.

Words are powerful. So, you must choose wisely. Thread carefully, to find the balance and bask in parlance. Words my channel to connect and be heard.

I listened to the professors and here I am. Honestly, I say that these great men paved the way, for my words to live and breathe through this channel to connect and to be heard.

## CHANCES

I do not want to care and share.
Or try to change the course of life.
Just listen to your heart and you will realize
that, in holding me close, you reveal parts of
you that I desire.

I do not want to care and share,
Taste, and then lose in haste
This wonderful feeling that I need, that may not
stay. If your future is already decided, do not
reveal parts that I desire.

I do not want to care and share.
Nor partake in the life of a tease.
Please, let not your human nature overtake the
need for you to know that no matter how right
this feels, this is just one pleasure that I must do
without. Do not reveal parts of you that I
desire.

## GRATITUDE

You, in my life, make a huge difference.
You laud my strengths and diminish my flaws.
You bring a ray of hope. You give my world a
new meaning. You align with my future. You
prove them all wrong by staying and giving.

You reaffirm my deepest conviction that I am someone more, rather than someone less.

## I YEARN TO LEARN

I may not know it all but there is so much I learnt from birth. With knowledge in
My girth, eyes twinkling with mirth, I yearn
To learn.
I may not know it all, but I tap into my subconscious and relate it to the conscious. All around me traces in places, answers to my puzzles. I yearn to learn.

I may not know it a. There is a reason for every season. Boundless depths, heights that seem unattainable. No matter how easy it may seem. There is something harder. I
yearn to learn.

I may not know it all, but I am taking it in my stride, finding balance, finding my niche, building a fortress far beyond the reach of mere mortals. I yearn to learn.

## WHAT THE FUTURE HOLDS

My dear friends. We may not know what the
future holds, but judging from stories of old, you
will never be left in the cold. Let life unfold.
The trickier it gets, the greater your
resolve. Solve every riddle that poses a hurdle.
Hasten your steps and fasten your belt.  Plan
and let life unfold.

For in our today lies tomorrow's strength.
shadows behind us are things of the past.
See the mirage ahead.
Plan, and let life unfold.

## GLOW

I like the glow; it is coming from the flow. You
can decide to take it slow, in the end, it will
show. The world will see the reason for the
glow, no matter how slow the flow. I will not
hide my glow. In the end, it is still going to
show.

HEARTBEAT

Every time you are near, I can hear my
heartbeat. Sometimes I fear as I listen. It
becomes clear, that you do not mean to
Scare but to show me that you care.


NEVER SAY NEVER

Even when I say never, I find myself ever falling
into one palaver or another. But even if it takes
forever, my obstacles will end up being my
lever.

NOTHING BUT THE TRUTH

I want you to know the truth. Nothing can save
you but the truth. Trace it back to the root. All
you will find is a young shoot.
Do not kick it with the boot. It is nothing but a
moot. When it all ends, I will break into a hoot,
song of the wise one and nothing but the truth.

## LOVE NOTES

In my heart there is a melody that breaks
Into a rhapsody. There is harmony as I am
lifted. This is not a parody but a testimony that
breaks the circle of melancholy.

## HEARTACHE

There was a gash in her heart.
It hurt, she cried, it bled.
There was a pain in her heart.
She was shaken, shattered, her heart bled.
Her heart hurt, the tears dried,
Then she tried to find all the pieces.
Still she bled, till it was time.
She knew, she must start anew.
She no longer bled but slowly the pain fled.

## TREE OF LOVE

On the tree of life, I found apples fresh,
ripe and appealing. Had I not been warned,
then my present predicament would have
been blamed on another.

Just like our first parents I found myself wanting
that which I was warned against but cannot
resist, juicy on the outside sour underneath.

From this same tree I am still plucking, hoping
that the next one I pluck would be the best
and my final pick.

My basket is filled with half bitten apples,
rotting away and I moving away.
Oh! I long to eat one more apple and eat it all.
It may be a fantasy, but this must be my final
pick. Call it faith or fate, the die is cast.


MY ALL AND ALL

The day I find him, the one who is ready to be
my friend for life. He will be my all and all. That
friend, who will not let me fall but call my name
in the dark, bringing me into the light.
In the dead of night, when the world sees the
side it chooses to see, I will follow that voice
and run with arms wide open, into the arms of
the one who is my all and all.

## ELUSION

I can understand when certain things elude
me. Like that call I am expecting. The look of
pride urging me to carry on.
The pat on my shoulder, the warm hug, the
expected ovation after hard work.
The tears of joy, the thrill of winning, the smell of
deception and moments of anxiety.

I can handle a whole range of emotions, but I
may never be able to decipher the abrupt
end of friendship. In what words can it be
explained? The demise of companionship and
of camaraderie. The broken chord of familiar
space and solace.
The dawn of mistrust. A realization that time
spent in friendship, has been a waste.

## CONSCIENCE

My mind is adrift, going through a rebirth. I
believe strongly that the mind, body, and spirit
are different yet connected.
It is easy to understand that we all exist in a
body controlled by our minds. The mind sets
the tone of what we accept and how we

conform. Often confused by deeply rooted thinking and beliefs.

Conscience stands in between, as the still small voice. It creeps up on men while they sleep or wide awake. It will not stop even when you want it to stop. It is what makes the guilty sit on edge and look over their shoulders. It is deeply rooted.

When you decide to kill it, you feel the chilly hands of coldness; the kind that makes you shiver and quiver and run when no one is in pursuit. It is there; no one can see it. It is silent yet loud and clear. It is deeply rooted.

## OPEN TO LOVE

I made a vow that I shall be open to love. I shall embrace it with open arms. I shall give it even when I do not receive it.
I shall not overlook it when I find it. I will respect it and let it grow. I shall not see it as a mystery a harbinger of misery.
I shall not see it as a myth but as a reality which lives and breathes in hearts, hearts aflame with

passion, on a mission, to engulf other hearts, to set the world on fire.

INDEX OF FIRST LINES

## J

Just because being
with you seems, 8

## M

My dear friend. Let
not (your)face be,
12
My dear friends, we
may not know, 17
My mind is adrift,
going through, 23

## O

On the tree of life,,
20
One beautiful day,
on my way to
Kilburn, by train, 2
Over two decades,
1

## S

Sometimes life is like
a holiday, 9

## T

The day I find him,
21
The power of touch
is a gift. The ability
to, 12
The way you talk is
like music to my
ears., 6
There is a stand I
have taken, a
decision I, 5
There was a gash in
her heart, 20
This new day gives
the pleasure of, 7
Today, I marry the
one I love, the
one, 5

## W

Words are my
passion, 14

## Y

You, in my life,
make a huge
difference, 16

Doubra Fufeyin: Friendship is Love

Printed in Great Britain
by Amazon

85711787R00031